Ancient EGYPT

MOMENTS IN HISTORY

BY SHIRLEY JORDAN

Perfection Learning®

Cover Illustration: Corbis/Christine Osborne

About the Author

Shirley Jordan is a retired elementary school teacher and principal. Currently a lecturer in the teacher-training program at California State University, Fullerton, California, she sees exciting things happening in the world of social studies. Shirley loves to travel—with a preference for sites important to U.S. history.

She has had more than 50 travel articles published in recent years. It was through her travels that she became interested in "moments in history," those ironic and little-known stories that make one exclaim, "I didn't know that!" Such stories are woven throughout her books.

Image credits: Art Today pp. 4 (top, middle), 5 (second, third, fourth), 6, 13 (top, middle), 14, 15, 16 (top), 18, 19, 21, 22, 23 (top, bottom), 25, 26, 27 (top), 28, 30, 31, 32, 35, 36 (bottom), 38 (bottom), 41, 42, 44, 45 (top), 46, 47 (bottom), 48, 49; Corbis pp. 7, 12 (top), 43, 45 (bottom), 51, 54 (bottom); Corel pp. 4 (bottom), 10, 11, 12 (bottom), 13 (bottom), 16 (bottom), 17 (middle, bottom), 23 (middle), 24, 27 (bottom), 29, 33, 34, 36 (top), 40, 47 (top, middle), 53; CyberPhoto pp. 3, 5 (first), 17 (top), 20, 37, 38 (top), 39, 50, 52, 54 (top)

Table of Contents

A Timeline of Important Events 4

Chapter 1. Egypt's Beginnings 7

Chapter 2. The Pharaoh 10

Chapter 3. Osiris and Isis 12

Chapter 4. Other Important Egyptians 14

Chapter 5. Home Life 21

Chapter 6. Time for a Feast 27

Chapter 7. The Nile River 30

Chapter 8. The Pyramids 33

Chapter 9. The Egyptians and Mathematics 37

Chapter 10. The Sphinx 39

Chapter 11. Honoring the Dead 40

Chapter 12. Two Famous Queens 48

Chapter 13. How We've Learned About the
Ancient Egyptians 50

Glossary 55

Index 56

A Timeline of Important Events

(Please note: Dates are approximate.
Names of kings may have various spellings.)

THE EARLY PERIOD

5000 B.C. **Nomads** make their homes on the Nile. Several kingdoms rule different parts of the river. Early forms of picture writing, or **hieroglyphics**, are scratched onto stone.

3100 B.C. King Menes of Upper Egypt conquers Lower Egypt. He becomes the first **pharaoh** of all Egypt. His government is in Memphis. History is recorded with hieroglyphics.

THE OLD KINGDOM

2700 B.C. The first pyramid is built. It is the Step Pyramid for King Djoser.

2500 B.C. It is the golden age of pyramids. The Great Pyramid is built for King Cheops. The pyramids at Giza are constructed.

THE FIRST INTERMEDIATE PERIOD

2230 B.C. There are several poor harvests in a row. Egypt breaks into smaller governments.

THE MIDDLE KINGDOM

2160 B.C. Thebes becomes the capital of Egypt. The pharaoh Mentuhotep unites Egypt again. This is a period of cultural glory.

THE SECOND INTERMEDIATE PERIOD

1674–
1575 B.C. Egypt is invaded by the Hyksos, a tribe from Asia. They introduce horses, **chariots,** and bronze.

THE NEW KINGDOM

1570 B.C. The Hyksos are driven out of Egypt.

1524–
1518 B.C. Pharaoh Thutmose I conquers Palestine and Syria.

1503–
1482 B.C. Hatshepsut is the daughter of Thutmose I. She married her weak brother, Thutmose II. She becomes Egypt's first female ruler.

1458 B.C.	Thutmose III conquers Syria and Palestine. The Egyptian kingdom is strong. He was called the Warrior King.
1374 B.C.	A pharaoh named Akhenaten tries to set up a new **supreme** god called Aten. His ideas are not popular.
1323 B.C.	The boy king, Tutankhamen, reigns for nine years.
1304– 1238 B.C.	This is the reign of Ramses II. He is probably pharaoh at the time of Moses.

THE LATE PERIOD ▪ ▪ ▪ ▪ ▪ ▪ ▪ ▪ ▪

525 B.C.	Egypt is conquered by the Persians. They build a **canal** to the Red Sea.
332 B.C.	Alexander the Great and his Macedonian (Greek) armies conquer Egypt and most of the known world. When Alexander dies, his general, Ptolemy, claims Egypt.
323–30 B.C.	The Ptolemies, a Greek dynasty, rule as pharaohs. Cleopatra is the last of them.
30 B.C.	Conquest by the Romans. Egypt becomes part of the Roman Empire.

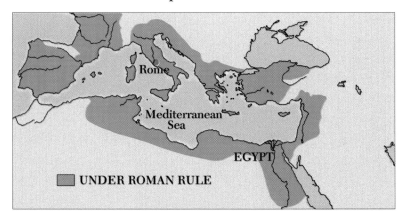

Rome

Mediterranean Sea

EGYPT

▨ UNDER ROMAN RULE

1
CHAPTER

Egypt's Beginnings

$\mathcal{T}$he lands of northern Africa were once a huge swamp. Then the soil began to dry out. This drying took hundreds of years.

After a while, tribes settled on the rich soil of the Nile Valley. These early settlers had been nomads. They moved from place to place. Now they had found a good land.

The nomads began to stay all year. And they felt safer with others around them. Some small communities were started along the Nile River. All these things happened more than 5,000 years ago.

Why was the soil along the Nile so rich?

Each summer, beginning in June, the mighty river flooded. The Nile flowed through Egypt for 600 miles. The entire river overflowed its banks.

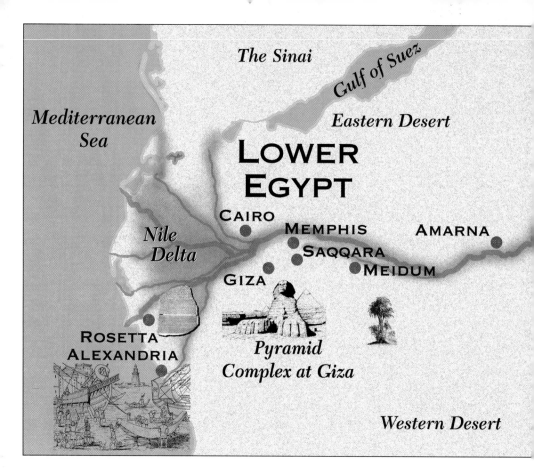

The Sinai

Gulf of Suez

Mediterranean Sea

Eastern Desert

LOWER EGYPT

CAIRO

MEMPHIS

AMARNA

SAQQARA

Nile Delta

GIZA

MEIDUM

Pyramid Complex at Giza

ROSETTA

ALEXANDRIA

Western Desert

In some places, the flood spread for only one mile. But in other places, the land was flat. The Nile could pour wet, new soil much farther in these flat lands. Such a flooded area might cover as many as 12 miles. About six miles on each side of the river.

Each year, the flood lasted about four months. Then the water went down. The river went back to its proper path.

Grasses and reeds had grown in the wet soil. They lined the riverbank. And they brought good fortune to the settlers.

Ducks, geese, and cranes came to feed. They built nests and raised their families. Fish crowded the waters of the Nile. This was the food the settlers were looking for.

Some of the communities grew into small kingdoms. Each one had some sort of leader. These kingdoms stretched along different parts of the river. For the most part, the people lived in peace for 2,000 years.

In about 3000 B.C., there was a king of Upper Egypt. His name

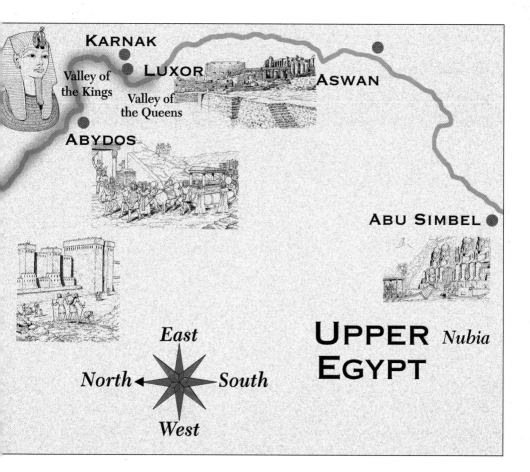

was Menes. (Some historians have given him the names of Narmer or Aha.) He ruled the area to the south. That's where the Nile Valley was very narrow.

Menes wanted his kingdom to join Lower Egypt. That was the northern land where the Nile River reached the Mediterranean Sea.

There was much more **fertile** land in the north. And Menes wanted the delta. That was the triangle of land where the river entered the Mediterranean.

He sent his army against the people of the north. In a short time, Menes conquered them. He was able to unite the kingdom of the north with the kingdom of the south.

He became the first king, or pharaoh, over all Egypt.

Menes was a good pharaoh. He built his capital at a city called Memphis. A civilization developed.

Men who could write, or scribes, kept records in pictures and codes. The pictures and codes were called *hieroglyphics*.

The Pharaoh

After Menes united the kingdom of Egypt, he became the first king, or pharaoh. Powerful leaders followed him on the throne for 3,000 years.

Every man, woman, and child in Egypt knew of the pharaoh's power. He was the most important man in the country. A mighty leader, he owned everything in the kingdom. When the pharaoh said something, his words became the law. But there were no laws that the pharaoh had to obey.

The people of Egypt believed he was a god. Only the most important Egyptians were allowed near him. They considered it a great honor just to kiss the dirt near his feet.

The pharaoh lived in a great palace. In fact, the title *pharaoh* came from two Egyptian words. They were *per* and *aa.* Together, they meant "great house." So *pharaoh* came to mean "one who lives in the great house."

Pharaohs were called by different names. Some of the names were "son of the sun god," "the good shepherd," or "the great warrior."

No matter what he was called, no one argued about a pharaoh's power. It was complete.

If you were the child of a pharaoh, you would live in a fine palace.

There would be many servants. Servants did nothing but wait on the pharaoh's family.

As a pharaoh's child, you would have dozens of sisters and brothers. It was common in those days for pharaohs to have many wives. The palace was a busy, active place.

Each pharaoh chose one of his wives to be "the great queen." She was especially honored in the palace. The other wives might be very jealous of her. They would be careful not to let that jealousy show.

But something else was more important about the great queen. Her oldest son had special power. He would be in line to be the next pharaoh. When his father died, he would sit on the throne. This was true even if the pharaoh had older sons by another wife.

If you were one of the pharaoh's sons, your mother might not be the great queen. But you would still be trained to be a leader. Perhaps you were headed for a job in Egypt's government.

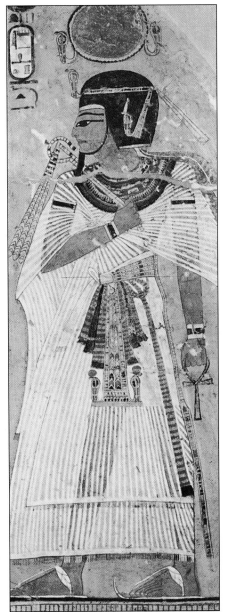

It would be important that you married the right young woman. Your parents would choose her for you.

It was common for children within the pharaoh's family to marry each other. You might marry a cousin or a half-sister—the child of one of the other wives. This was considered a good thing for the pharaoh. It kept all the power in the ruler's family.

When a pharaoh's family grew large and strong, no one dared go against any of the members. One after another, they would take the throne. Such a family group was a *dynasty.* That means a line of leaders all from one family. In its 3,000 years of history, ancient Egypt had 31 such dynasties.

Ancient Egyptians believed their pharaoh was a god. They also believed in many other gods. Read on for one of the earliest and best-known stories.

3

CHAPTER

Osiris and Isis

Osiris and Isis were favorite gods of the Egyptians. Osiris was thought to be the grandson of the sun god, Re.

The Egyptians believed he had been one of the earliest kings. He was known as a kind and fair ruler who looked after the growth of plants. In their drawings of Osiris, ancient artists showed him with green skin.

Isis was the wife of Osiris. She was also his sister and another grandchild of Re. Osiris and Isis were happy together. They had a son named Horus.

The Egyptians believed an interesting story about Osiris. While he was king, his brother, Set, became jealous of him. Set was a very evil god. He tricked Osiris into getting into a box. Then Set threw the box into the sea.

Isis found the box. But Set stole the body of Osiris. He cut it up into 14 pieces. Then Set scattered those pieces all over Egypt.

The faithful Isis searched and searched for her husband. At last, she found all the pieces.

With the help of the jackal-headed god Anubis, she put Osiris's body back together. When he was back in one piece, Isis brought Osiris back to life.

Having once been dead, however, Osiris could no longer rule the living. So he became King of the Dead.

Horus, the son of Osiris and Isis, went after Set. He fought his evil uncle. It was a bitter battle. While they were fighting, Set put out one of Horus's eyes. But young Horus fought back bravely. He killed Set. He got even for the death of his father. And Horus became a king of Egypt.

Ancient temple paintings tell this story. Osiris often wears the coned pharaoh's hat of Upper Egypt. He holds a **shepherd's crook** and a **thresher's flail.**

The Egyptians called Isis "the mother of all things." In drawings, she is shown in human form. She wears a crown made of cow's horns. A sun disk appears between the horns. Isis holds the *ankh*, the symbol of life, in her right hand. In her left is a staff.

Horus is remembered in paintings too. The magic eye, or Eye of Horus, is a sign of the sun or moon. It means good luck. It is a protector against evil spirits.

CHAPTER 4

Other Important Egyptians

The pharaoh couldn't be everywhere at once. So other powerful people helped him. There were priests and generals. There were government officials. And there were those who owned a great deal of land.

The pharaoh was careful that these people approved of his actions. He could never let them think he was weak. He was afraid they might start small kingdoms of their own.

The power in ancient Egypt was like a pyramid. The pharaoh was at the very top. His scribes, generals, and other important helpers might be partway down the pyramid. And all the **peasants** would form the wide base.

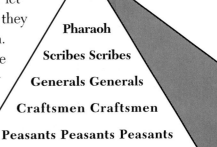

Pharaoh

Scribes Scribes

Generals Generals

Craftsmen Craftsmen

Peasants Peasants Peasants

Slaves Slaves Slaves Slaves

THE SCRIBES

Sometimes the pharaoh was too far away to make a decision. In that case, it was made by his scribes.

If you were the child of a scribe, you would be very proud.

Your father would be one of the record keepers and managers for the pharaoh. He would have a fine office built of sun-dried mud bricks. People would come to his door to ask for favors.

14

Each small village had a scribe to collect the taxes. Sometimes he had to settle boundary lines. Or serve as a priest. Or design public buildings.

Every few years, the pharaoh might think a battle was near. He would send an order to his scribes. They would sign up soldiers from the villages to fight.

As a young man growing up in Egypt, you might hope to be a scribe someday. It would help if your father was one.

If your family was noble with great landholdings, that would be good too. Then you might be chosen to attend a scribes' school. It would be in Thebes. That was near the pharaoh's palace.

Your father, as a scribe, could not pass down his job to you. But he could help you be chosen for the scribe training. If you did well in your studies, the job would be yours.

You would have to work hard. At school, you would sit long hours on a hard stone bench. And no one was allowed to speak. (Except the teacher!)

You would study *surveying*, or measuring land. There would be classes in architecture and history. The pharaoh might even order all the scribes to learn poetry.

Writing would be very important. You would have to know the 23 letters of the Egyptian alphabet. You would learn 700 written signs to represent sounds.

At first, you would write on stones or wood. *Papyrus,* the special paper made from river reeds, was too precious.

Only after you had learned to write well would you use papyrus. After the writing was done, the sheet of papyrus paper could be rolled up and saved.

To be a scribe, you would have to be good at keeping records.

In ancient Egypt, very few women and girls learned to read and write. But *Egyptologists,* the people who study ancient Egypt, found a surprise. They studied the writing and pictures left behind. And they discovered a word in the ancient language that meant "woman scribe"!

People still don't know much about these educated females. We don't know what they really did. Or how many there might have been.

THE GOD THOTH

The moon god Thoth was believed to control all learning. He was the inventor of writing and speech. And he was the protector of the scribes.

The Egyptians had libraries. They believed that Thoth took care of them.

He was looked upon as the god who controlled the science of numbers, weights, and measures. The Egyptians were advanced in mathematics. And Thoth was one of the most respected gods.

The people also believed Thoth had great magical powers. They thought he could heal. And that he controlled the success of physicians.

He is usually portrayed as a bird, the ibis. Less often, he is shown as a baboon.

THE CRAFTSMEN

Many Egyptian objects that have survived since ancient times are the work of craftsmen. There were craftsmen such as metalworkers, jewelers, potters, and glassmakers.

The work of women, spinning and weaving, produced fine cloth. We see it in hieroglyphic paintings. But the cloth rotted away. No one has any now.

So powerful were the pharaohs that some of them kept whole villages of craftsmen near their tombs. They created the decorations needed there.

METALWORKING

Egypt, especially between the Nile River and the Red Sea, was rich in precious metals such as gold and silver. It contained large mines filled with glowing stones.

The craftsmen were masters of working with copper and bronze too. And the warm glow of these metals was very popular with wealthy people.

Gold was one of the most valued metals of all. Solid gold objects were made only for the pharaoh and a few of

the very rich. Some pharaohs have been found with solid gold mummy masks. But for others who were not so rich, objects were *gilded*, or covered with a thin outer gold layer.

Weapons for war were made by the metalworkers. Daggers were shaped of copper or bronze. Strong ax heads came from bronze.

First, the metals had to be heated to burn off the impurities. This process was *smelting*. Then the craftsmen cooled the metal. They hammered it into the shape they wanted.

Other times, they poured the liquid metal into molds. Either way, there was much work to be done. The molded object had to be scraped, rubbed, and polished for many hours.

JEWELRY

Silver was the most popular jewelry metal. It was also the most costly.

Another popular metal was *electrum*. That was a combination of gold and silver. Women loved it.

Electrum was often used for belts, anklets, and bracelets. The metal would be decorated with curled shapes that held precious stones like amethyst or turquoise.

POTTERY

The Egyptians made pots and jars from the mud of the Nile. Just like they used the mud to make bricks for their houses. There is

evidence that these ancient people had developed a simple potter's wheel.

After trampling the Nile mud into a paste, the potter shaped it into vases and jars. Then he baked it hard in the tall, hot **kilns.**

Besides household dishes and pots, the potter made animal forms. These were used as house decorations.

Before heating the clay figure, the potter coated it with a glassy substance. It was called *faience*. The finished piece of art was handsome. And it was long-lasting.

GLASSMAKING

Glass was made by mixing a large amount of sand and small amounts of lime, soda, and other materials. The Egyptian glassmaker put the mixture in clay pots. He heated the mixture in a furnace until it was like a thick syrup.

The ancient Egyptians were the first to successfully make glass. Everything needed was present—sand, soda, and wood fuel for the ovens.

There is evidence that craftsmen in 1500 B.C. pressed glass into open molds. They learned how to color glass. And they made jewelry, jars, and tiny jugs.

A big step forward in glassmaking was the blowpipe. An **artisan** invented it in about 300 B.C.

Egypt was already the world's center for glassmaking. And the craftsmen began producing glassware that even the less wealthy could afford.

THE PRIESTS

If you were the son of a priest, you would have many things to learn.
The job of priest was usually handed down from father to son.

Every town had at least one temple. You would have special duties at that temple.

You would learn that the priest got up early each day. He shaved

and washed carefully. Then he went to the temple. He carefully entered a small *sanctuary*, or holy room. There would be a separate **shrine** for each of the town's gods.

At the shrine, the priest took out the statue of a god. He sprinkled water on it and changed its clothing. Then he offered the god some food and drink. He repeated the process for each god's statue. Then he put the statues back

THE GOD AMON

Amon was the Egyptians' most important god. He was also known as Amon-Re. That means "Amon the Sun."

In paintings he had a human body. He wore a headdress with two large feathers on top.

Amon's main center of worship was at Thebes in Upper Egypt. In temples there, he was shown in paintings with his wife Mut.

into their shrines with the doors open.

He left the temple, wiping away his footprints as he went. When the sun set, he returned to the temple. He closed the door to the temple until the next morning.

THE PEASANTS

If you were the child of a peasant, your life would be hard.

You would be part of the largest group of ancient Egyptians. Your family would work from dawn to sundown. It would take that much work just to have enough to eat.

Chances are good that your father would be a farmer. He might plant a small part of a rich man's land. When the crops were ready, the whole family would harvest them.

The owner of the land would get most of the crops. Your family would have only a small portion of the wheat, barley, or flax. Then your father would pay taxes on his portion.

In summer, the fields were flooded by the Nile. That was when the pharaoh or another very rich man built his tomb.

The peasants were paid to work on the tombs. It was hard work. There was much heavy lifting. The sun burned down on the workers. They became thirsty and tired.

But building tombs was the only work in the summer. So at least the peasants could put food on the table.

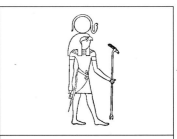

THE GOD RE

Re (sometimes called Ra) was the god of the sun. He was worshiped as "the father of fathers." And also as "the mother of mothers."

Just as Osiris was the god of the dead, Re was the god of the living. The Egyptians believed that each pharaoh was a son of Re.

He is shown in paintings with a human form. Sometimes he has the head of a falcon and a human body. And he is shown carrying a sun disk as his symbol.

THE SLAVES

The Nile River passed through 600 miles of Egypt. So it was hard to protect all the borders of the kingdom. Sometimes the pharaoh had to send armies to fight.

If the pharaoh's men won the war, they could claim prisoners. These prisoners would then become Egypt's slaves. And their children would be slaves too.

If you were the child of a slave in ancient Egypt, you would not feel very hopeful.

Being a slave was worse than being a peasant. Peasants were free. And they had to work hard to live. But slaves worked even harder. And they were the property of the pharaoh.

When slaves cut the crops, no portion belonged to them. They hoped that the pharaoh would provide some food and shelter.

Home Life

If you were the son or daughter of a rich Egyptian, your family would live in a large house.

Your house would be surrounded by gardens. The servants would carry water from the river to water the plants.

There would be a stable for horses. And other buildings where the household servants lived.

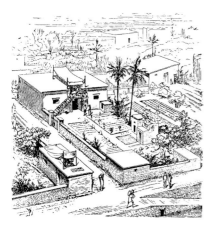

Some houses were built with flat roofs. The cooking was done up there. Otherwise, cooking was done in a special mud brick building nearby.

Your father would own farmland. There the peasants could grow crops such as barley and wheat. Your father would let them use his fields. Then they would give him a share of their harvest. A *steward*, a man good with numbers, made sure that the peasants brought your father his share.

Not all the peasants on your father's land grew crops. Some raised cattle or geese. The steward made sure your father got his share of these animals too.

Like all Egyptian homes, your family's house would be built of mud bricks. Only temples and pyramids were made from stone.

When your father first came to the land, he would have hired workmen. Their job would have been to make the bricks.

To do that, the men mixed mud with sand or straw. Before the bricks could be used for walls, they had to be dried in the sun. Until they were hard as rocks.

Once the house was finished, the walls were painted with a thin mixture called *whitewash*. When floors were added, they were built above the level of the ground. This made it hard for snakes to crawl in.

While he was helping build a house, a workman was paid by the day. Each morning, he was given three loaves of bread, two jugs of beer, and a bunch of onions to eat.

It was very hot. And the worker wore nothing but a short linen skirt, tied in front. *Linen* was a cloth made from the flax plant grown in the Nile Valley.

Your house would have windows but no glass. The windows were cut high up on the wall. They let in light. But not the hot sunshine. The high windows also let the heated air near the roof escape to the outside.

The Egyptians used trees wisely for shade. Trees were also important for food. Sycamore, fig, and acacia trees were planted near houses.

Egyptian homes did not have much furniture. Those who could afford it used low chairs and tables of wood.

Folding stools—with legs carved in the form of animals or birds—were very popular with the rich. Chair seats were sometimes covered with leather.

Leather furniture was not for servants and poor people, however. They sat on bright-colored mats or cushions.

Your house might be cool and shady inside. But you and your friends would spend much of the day outdoors. To keep cool, most children had shaved heads.

As a child in a wealthy family, you would not have hard work to do. You could play ball games with the other children. Or you could spin tops. When it was too hot outside, you might choose board games, toy animals, or dolls.

If you were a boy of 10 or 11, you would begin to learn other things. You would practice shooting arrows or fighting with a sword. You would need to know these skills.

Someday, you might have to defend your home from invaders. You would learn these things because Egyptian boys married when they were about 14.

If you were a daughter, you would learn many things from your mother.

Before long, you would have to run a household and direct servants. You would also have to look your best. Young women married when they were about 12.

All Egyptians were very clean. House servants would spend much time carrying water for bathing and washing clothes. They would make a sticky paste soap to wash dirt from your skin.

Many Egyptian women shaved their arms and legs. They used bronze razors. Your mother would teach you and your sisters to pluck your eyebrows with tweezers.

You would learn to dip a small ivory stick into a bottle of black, sticky stuff called *kohl*. With this, you would draw a black line around each eye.

You would not have to guess where this black line was going. For the Egyptians had mirrors. They were made of bronze. The bronze was polished to a high shine. Then it gave a good reflection. These early mirrors worked well.

Some young women were too poor to own a mirror. They looked at themselves in standing pools of water.

You would also learn to paint your face and body with *ochre*. This iron ore came from the soil. It might be yellow, orange, or red. Red was the most popular and expensive color.

As a young girl, you would learn to mix the ochre with a bit of oil from olive trees. You could spread the color on your eyelids, cheeks, and lips.

You, your mother, and your sisters would use *henna*. That was a red dye made from a plant grown near Egypt. You would use henna to decorate the palms of your hands, the soles of your feet, and your fingernails and toenails.

Your dress would be a loose linen robe. Over the robe would go a beaded collar. You'd wear brightly colored bracelets. And long, dangling earrings. Both of your parents would wear jewelry. They would wear as much as they could afford.

A servant might spend an hour fixing your freshly washed hair into narrow braids.

Your mother, however, would have a stiff, heavy wig of such braids. First, she would paint her face and body. Then her personal attendant would lift the wig into place.

Men and women who did not wear wigs often curled their hair. If it turned gray, they colored it.

When it was time to leave the house, your mother would put on a soft, open pair of sandals. They were curled up in front to keep the dirt out.

As a young Egyptian, you would love good food. Even poor people had a healthy diet. Everyone ate plenty of fruit, vegetables, and bread. The barley the Egyptians grew was used for making bread and beer.

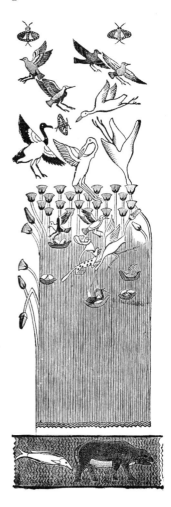

Rich people drank beer too. They also liked wine. It was made from their farms' grapes. The juice was stored in clay jars while it changed into wine.

Fish came from the Nile. And meat came from the cattle raised on large farms. The meat was roasted with herbs and spices. Ducks and geese were dried in the sun so their meat would not spoil.

After the summer floods, crops were planted in the rich black soil. As the crops came up, small boys scared away the birds from the young plants. Your young brother might have that job.

Everything grew well. It was even possible to plant and harvest two crops in a year. This kept the farmers very busy.

All winter, the level of the fields was higher than the Nile River. The workers on your father's farm used a tool called a *shaduf* to water the crops. The shaduf worked like a pulley. With it, buckets of water could be lifted from the river. It took many servants to move this water from the river to the fields.

Your family would be large. People married young and had many children. There were many illnesses. Some babies died when they were very young. So the family wanted many children to be sure some of them grew up.

Houses in ancient Egypt became very crowded. Girls stayed home until they were married.

The head of a household also had to take care of aunts and sisters who had not married. Grandparents often lived in the house too.

Women could own property in ancient Egypt. But they still lived under the control of their fathers and husbands. Divorce was legal. But it rarely happened.

Paintings in Egyptian tombs show families working and playing together. Historians have decided that family life in ancient Egypt was usually happy. And always busy.

THE GODDESS HATHOR

Hathor was the Egyptian goddess of heaven, joy, music, love, birth, and death. She was often called upon to protect children. Mothers prayed to her to bless their childbirth.

Sometimes she was described as the Lady of Terror. She destroyed the enemies of the sun god. Hathor is often pictured as a cow.

26

CHAPTER

Time for a Feast

The Egyptians loved parties. Most years, there was plenty of food to share. And many servants to prepare it.

Hepeth, 10, and his sister Narah, 12, were excited. Their parents had invited most of the town to a feast. The harvest had been good that year. The gods had been kind to their family. And to all the Nile Valley.

All day, servants roasted ducks and geese over an open fire. Piles of fruits and vegetables were brought from the gardens. Baskets of figs came from the fig trees.

The slaves had mixed grain into dough all night. Fresh baked breads filled huge baskets. Hepeth and Narah could hardly wait. The smell of all that fresh bread made them hungry.

"How much longer before the feast?" Hepeth asked. He wished his personal servant hadn't dressed him so early. "I don't like having to keep clean."

His sister frowned at him. "Neither do I," she said. "But I won't complain. Mother let me dye my hands and feet this time. And she promised I could wear a perfume cone on my head next year."

She showed Hepeth the red coloring on her palms. "Mother says I'm old enough to think about a husband. I think she and Father have someone in mind."

"Who? Is he from our village?"

"They won't tell me," Narah said. "But I'm certainly old enough to marry. Don't you think so?"

Before Hepeth could answer, the two of them heard the first guests.

Friends and neighbors soon filled the courtyard. Hepeth and Narah's father and mother greeted each arrival.

How beautiful Mother looks, thought Narah.

The servants passed fine wines. The grapes had come from the family vineyards. Servants had been crushing the grapes and filling the clay jars for weeks.

The roasted ducks and geese were brought on huge platters. Breads of many grains were offered. Honey from the family's bees sweetened everything.

Like all ancient Egyptians, everyone at the party ate with his or her hands.

Narah passed behind her brother. "Try not to drip on your best tunic," she whispered.

Narah decided not to eat much. Perhaps her future husband was among the guests. He must never see her with spots on her linen garment!

People had come dressed in their finest clothes. They all wore jewelry. The bright sun sparkled off the gems.

Each guest wore a perfume cone on his or her head. These cones melted as the party went on. Soon all the guests were drenched in sweet-smelling oils.

Married couples sat together at the party. Those not married were separated. There was a group of boys in one place. And a group of girls in another.

Hepeth and Narah's parents gave all the children—boys and girls alike—flower necklaces. They gave them flowers for their hair too.

In ancient Egypt, it was considered rude not to eat too much. A good guest was one who ate until he was sick. Many drank too much of the host's wine. They had to be helped home by the servants. This was considered the polite way to act.

The Egyptians loved to talk. They discussed crops, jewelry, and families. Servants passed among them offering more food and wine.

Singers and dancers performed in the middle of the courtyard. Musicians played harps, pipes, lutes, drums, and tambourines.

Narah was very excited. Her father had hired acrobats this time.

No one was in a hurry to go home. After all the food had been offered, the servants passed trays of sweet breads and rolls. Many of them had walnuts, dates, and honey.

Narah was too full for the sweets. But she noticed that Hepeth and his friends ate and ate until the party ended.

The Nile River

Egypt's lands stretched far from each side of the Nile. But most Egyptians lived near the river. There was no easy way to live in the dry stretches of desert.

THE RIVER AND THE HUNTER

The Nile was the source of most of Egypt's food. Fishermen wove nets from the reeds that grew along the river banks. With these nets, they could bring in a good catch. Some of the fish were eaten right away. The rest could be smoked and kept for a later time.

The river brought other animals for food. Ducks, geese, and cranes still flocked along the banks. Hunters caught those in nets too. Or they threw sticks at the fowl to bring them down.

Sometimes the men went after larger prey. Hippopotamuses and crocodiles hid in the marshes. Brave hunters tracked them. Their weapons were sharpened metal points mounted on long wooden poles.

THE RIVER AND THE FARMER

Fish and animals were fine. But the Nile's greatest gift was the fertile farmland. Nephret, a farmer's son, knew this.

Every June, he watched the Nile rise. It flooded over its banks. And it covered his father's fields.

For four hot months, the water soaked the land. The soil turned rich and black. Nephret watched the river spread out layers of the earth that had filled its floodwaters.

Then the water level returned to normal. And it was time to plow the rich, moist soil.

Nephret helped his father plant the seeds. The early nomads had planted whatever they could find. But now, hundreds of years later, Nephret's father chose corn, barley, and flax.

After planting, the farmers took care of the **dikes,** canals, and ditches. These brought water from the river to the fields during the dry season.

By March, the fields were ready for harvest. Men, women, and children worked together.

Nephret's father and the other men used **sickles** to cut the stalks of grain. This year, Nephret used a sickle too.

The women and children bundled the stalks into **sheaves.** Then they went back over the ground, *gleaning.* That means that they picked up anything the **reapers** had missed. They filled baskets with what they had gleaned.

Each farm's boundaries were marked with large stones. Government officials inspected the fields at harvest time. They made sure these markers had not been moved. Taxes were gathered according to the size of the fields.

Nephret's father and the other farmers had to swear they had not changed any of the boundaries.

THE RIVER AS A HIGHWAY

The Nile River flowed gently northward through the heart of Egypt. To travel north, a boat could float with the current. To go south, it had to be pushed with poles or rowed with oars.

The Nile was as useful as a modern highway. Large- and medium-sized boats carried goods from one town to another. Near shore, fishermen wove small boats out of reeds and floated out to the best fishing grounds.

Paintings found in Egyptian tombs have shown how well advanced Egyptian boatbuilding was. But those with their own boats were rich men.

Wood was scarce in Egypt. It had to be imported from the east coast of the Mediterranean Sea. It came from an area called Byblos. That was in what is now the country of Lebanon. The finest boats were built in a large dockyard at Memphis.

Most boats on the Nile were of a style called the punt. Pilots stood in the **bow** and measured the depth of the water with a weighted line. In the **stern,** another sailor used a long oar as a rudder.

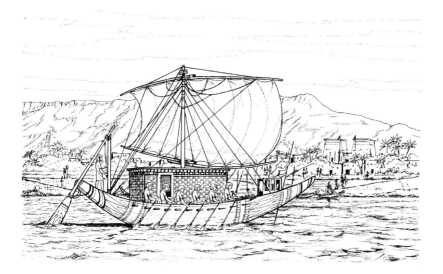

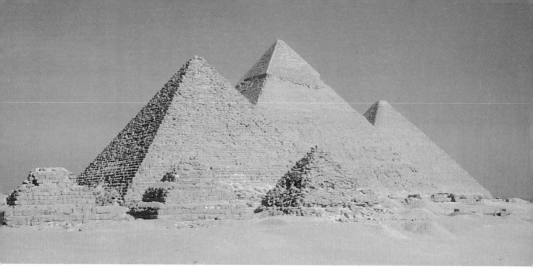

The Pyramids

During Egypt's first dynasty, people began to replace reed huts with brick buildings. Then, brick tombs, called *mastabas*, were built for important officials. They were built in the most important cemetery at Memphis.

These were big tombs with flat tops. Inside were storage rooms filled with goods. They were near the burial chamber.

When a king of those times died, some of his servants were killed and buried nearby. That way, the Egyptians believed, their spirits could continue to serve him in his new life.

THE FIRST PYRAMIDS ARE BUILT

If you lived in ancient Egypt, you might take a trip on the Nile.

Perhaps you would have traveled to see the great pyramids. When the river was flooded, its waters came very close to them.

They were built long, long ago. Very early in the history of ancient Egypt.

It was during this time that a very smart man named Imhotep was born. Some consider him the world's first genius.

Imhotep was probably the one who discovered how to build with stone. He drew the plans for the Step Pyramid at Saqqara. It was the first pyramid built in Egypt. It was begun in 2630 B.C.

Like the other pyramids, the Step Pyramid had more than one use. It was built to be the tomb of King Djoser. The people went there to worship the spirit, or *ka*, of the dead king.

The mummy of Djoser was buried under the pyramid. There were six layers of rock over his body. Unfortunately, robbers were able to break in. Modern Egyptologists found it empty.

In the fourth dynasty, King Snofru built two pyramids. They had straight sides. One of them changed direction halfway up. No one knows why. It is known as the Bent Pyramid.

Snofru was a kind ruler. The people were happy with the way he ran Egypt.

But the pharaoh that came after him, Cheops (or Khufu), was cruel. He ruled the people strictly. And he wanted a great deal of power. He had the Great Pyramid at Giza built for him.

Two other pharaohs from his dynasty built huge pyramids at Giza. Those kings were named Khephren and Menkaura.

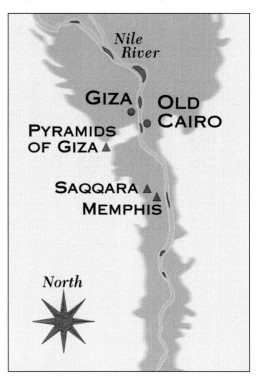

Over time, the tombs of queens, princesses, and important officials were also located near the great pyramids.

Treasures found in the pyramids and tombs show how advanced the ancients were. Medical books were buried there. Papers showing mathematics, astronomy, and engineering were also found.

Of course, the building of a pyramid took a great deal of knowledge. And a great deal of labor.

THE LABORERS

During flood season, there was little for farmers to do. So that was a good time for big projects. Each year, craftsmen and peasants were rounded up for this work.

It was backbreaking work. The Great Pyramid at Giza contains 2,300,000 blocks of stone. Each weighs between 2 and 15 tons!

During flood time, these huge blocks were taken by barge to the edge of the desert. The blocks were then tied onto crude wagons, or *sledges*. Hundreds of men dragged these sledges over wooden rollers.

Ramps made from mud sloped up to the pyramid. The men pulled the sledges—with the huge blocks on top—up these ramps.

As many as 100,000 men may have worked for 20 flood seasons. That's what it took to build *each* of the biggest pyramids.

THE DECLINE OF THE AGE OF PYRAMIDS

In later years, pharaohs still built pyramids. But they were not as large.

The Nile was not always good to the people. For many years, the floods were not as high. This meant less land for planting. There were *famines*, times when food was scarce.

By the 12th dynasty, the finest pyramid-making skills were gone. Buildings of this period were poorly built. They were not carefully decorated.

Artists used their skills in other ways, however. Now came a period of high-quality work on statues. Many statues showed the importance of family life. Some showed husbands and wives with their arms around each other.

In the years that followed, Egypt had some strong rulers. And some successful years. Never again, however, were structures like the pyramids built.

THE GOD IMHOTEP

Imhotep was not like the other Egyptian gods. He had been a real man of ancient Egypt. He lived about 2700 B.C. Imhotep was the chief assistant, or vizier, to King Djoser.

As one of the first doctors in the ancient world, he was very famous. When he died, the Egyptians made him one of their gods. A god of healing.

Imhotep was not just a doctor. He was also an architect, engineer, and statesman. And he designed the Step Pyramid at Saqqara.

The Egyptians and Mathematics

The Egyptians knew a lot about numbers. There was no zero in their counting system. But there was a symbol for *10*. Egyptians knew how to count by tens.

They didn't use numbers such as *2* through *9*. So the number *35* was written in symbols as "10+10+10+1+1+1+1+1."

These ancient people could multiply and divide whole numbers. And they knew how to reduce simple fractions. They invented a system of fractions like ½, ¼, and ¹⁄₁₀. Then they built them up to more difficult ones, such as ¾ and ⁷⁄₁₀.

The Egyptians were the first to measure their land by surveying it. Floodwaters washed away boundaries each year. So farms had to be measured again before they were planted.

The surveyors measured distances by using knots in a string. With the knots evenly spaced apart, they could stretch out the string. They counted the knots to figure distance.

One of their most important measurements was the *cubit*. That was the length of a man's arm. (From his elbow to the end of the middle finger.)

During the 500-year period called the Old Kingdom, the Egyptians were busy. They finished more than 20 major pyramids.

They were able to build these pyramids with great skill. They could find the area of things. And they could determine the volume.

Knowing about volume was important. That's because of the great weight of the pyramid stones.

At the Great Pyramid of Giza, each block weighed at least 5,000 pounds. The Egyptians worked to form a pyramid out of more than 2 million blocks. And each block had to be shaped just right. So it would fit with the others.

The Egyptians were the first people to work with geometry and algebra. Books on mathematics have been found in the tombs. They were written on papyrus leaves.

They were also astronomers. They could tell the difference between the planets and the stars. And they worked out a calendar of 365 days. It was much like ours.

10
CHAPTER

The Sphinx

A sphinx was a special kind of Egyptian statue. It showed a lion's body. But it did not have a lion's head. Usually it had the head of a man—a pharaoh.

Each sphinx was carved from one huge piece of rock.

The Egyptians thought the sphinx was a form of the sun god Re. The figure was believed to be a symbol of royal power.

A long row of sphinxes stands near a cluster of temples at Karnak. Each sphinx has the head of a ram. Under the ram's chin stands a king. The king's feet are between the lion's giant front paws.

This row of sphinxes stretches all the way from the ancient temples at Karnak to a canal miles away.

THE GREAT SPHINX

When most people talk about the Sphinx, they mean a special one. That one is called the Great Sphinx. It is near the pyramids at Giza. It seems to be guarding the three largest pyramids there. These are the ones honoring Cheops, Khephren, and Menkaura.

The Great Sphinx is 241 feet long. (It would cover about 80 yards of a football field.) Its tallest parts are 65 feet high, about like a six-story building. So it must have been carved out of one truly *big* piece of rock. The rock was limestone.

The front of the Great Sphinx faces east to honor Re, the sun god. That's where the sun comes up in the morning. It is likely the ancient Egyptians did this to honor Re.

The face is probably that of the mighty pharaoh Khephren. His pyramid tomb is just behind the Sphinx.

The Great Sphinx was worshiped as a sun god. So a smaller temple was built nearby. Pilgrims could leave their offerings to the sun god there.

The Great Sphinx and the pyramids at Giza are what visitors remember most about Egypt.

Honoring the Dead

If you lived in ancient Egypt, you would learn great respect for the dead.

Every Egyptian wanted to live forever. People believed that a well-treated **corpse** would someday awaken. Then he would begin a new life.

All large towns had a *necropolis*. That was a "city" of the dead. It had streets of tombs instead of houses.

Death was important to the Egyptians. So *embalmers*, the men who prepared a body after death, were greatly respected. They knew how to prepare a mummy.

Let's meet Ranu. He was the son of an embalmer. Ranu was learning to be an embalmer too. As training, he was one of his father's student helpers.

A rich and important man of the village had died. He had lived about 40 years. (That was about as long as the average Egyptian lived.) The man's family had enough money to honor him with a proper burial. So they had come to Ranu's father.

Like all Egyptians, the family believed this man had a *ba*, or soul. He also had a *ka*, an invisible twin. In giving him a proper burial, both the ba and the ka had to be honored.

"His ba and ka have left the body," Ranu's father explained. "They are waiting to live in his tomb. The ba will stay in contact with his living family members. And all his friends."

"What will happen to the ka?" asked Ranu.

"The ka has a special job," his father answered. "We will finish

preparing his body. Then this man will travel to another world. He will live with the gods and goddesses. A boat will take him there. The ka travels back and forth from the body to the other world."

40

"So the ba and ka still return to the body sometimes?"

"Yes, son," his father answered. "And that is why they must be able to recognize the body. You will see. We must finish making the body into a mummy. And then it will look much the way this man did in life."

Early the next day, Ranu followed his father to his workshop. It was just out of town. It was in the desert area near the tombs of the necropolis.

Ranu was very excited. He had not been allowed in the workshop before.

Soon a priest arrived. He prepared a ceremony for the beginning of the **mummification.**

The priest chanted. He made hand signs over the body. Ranu's father and some helpers joined in the chanting. Young Ranu tried to follow along with the words. But it was not easy this first time.

The ceremony ended with the priest casting a spell over the workshop. Now it was time to work on the body.

First, the inner organs had to be removed. Ranu watched, wide-eyed. His father took out a long hook with a handle. He pulled the brain out through the dead man's nose.

A helper gathered up the parts to throw them away.

"We do not save the brain," Ranu's father said. "It has no value."

Ranu's father worked on the head.

An assistant made a slit deep into the left side of the body. Soon he and another helper had removed the liver, lungs, stomach, and intestines.

But they did not remove the heart. That was left in place.

Now Ranu had a job. He brought four containers. They were called *canopic jars.* Then he watched his father wrap, or *embalm,* each of the inner organs. He wrapped them in *natron,* a chemical powder.

The man's embalmed liver went into one canopic jar. The jar was shaped like a vase. Its lid was a mask of Imsety. He was the god who protected the liver.

Each of the other organs had its own jar. And each of those had a different god's mask for a top. The lungs were protected by the god Hapy. The stomach by Duamutef. And the intestines by Qebhsenuef.

Ranu carefully carried the four jars, one by one, to a safe corner. It was an honor to do such important work.

Meanwhile, Ranu's father worked on the body. His assistants made small linen bundles of the natron. They stuffed these inside the body. Natron dried away fluids.

"Many years ago," Ranu's father began, "our people learned that a dried-out body would last for many years. In those days, they did it by digging into the hot sand. And burying the corpse a short distance below ground."

"Couldn't animals dig it up?" asked Ranu.

"That was one of the problems," his father answered. "And families wanted to bury possessions with their loved ones. Just as we do in the tombs now.

"Often, robbers dug up the treasures. They kept them for themselves."

Ranu's father scowled and shook his head. "Sometimes they took the body too."

This is important work I'm learning, thought Ranu. I'm proud to follow Father. Embalmers make sure people don't have to worry about the bodies of those they love.

The workers were gathered around a wooden board. They had lifted the natron-covered body onto it. Now they were stacking other wood

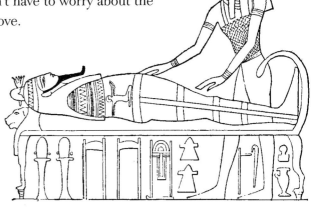

blocks under the board where the head rested. Soon the whole body was slanted, with the feet downward.

"The body will dry out," Ranu's father said. "Fluids will drip downward. Go get one of those old brown jars in the corner, my son. Put it below the feet of the corpse. It will catch the dripping."

Ranu secured the jar in place. His father chanted over it. Then he told Ranu it was time to go home. "There is nothing more to do with this body until 40 days have passed."

During the next weeks, Ranu made three more trips to his father's workshop. Five other bodies were being prepared. He wanted to study the tasks.

Each trip, he stood over the body of the rich man. It was the first mummy he had helped with. And he was very interested.

The 40 days of waiting passed slowly.

The time was finally up. Ranu could hardly wait. Now he would learn the next steps in mummification. He hurried with his father to the workshop. The other embalmers had just arrived.

His father brushed aside the natron. He opened the cut in the side of the corpse. He pulled out the cloth sacks.

The body was dry. Ranu could see how much it had shrunk.

His father handed him a sponge and nodded. Proudly, Ranu joined the older embalmers. They sponged the body clean. And they brushed it with oils.

Next they rubbed the corpse with ointments and spices. Hollow places were left where the natron sacks had been. Those were stuffed with bundles of spices.

Ranu's father finished some other important jobs. He plugged the eye sockets with linen cloth. He closed the eyelids. Then he stirred up a jar of beeswax and filled the nostrils.

After sewing up the cut in the side of the body, he covered it with a metal plate. The plate had the Eye of Horus on it.

Members of the family of the dead man arrived. They brought jewels they wanted to send with the body into its new life. Gold and precious stones soon decorated the corpse's arms, ankles, neck, and waist.

Now it was time to wrap the body. Ranu's father gave him a special job to do. He showed Ranu how to wrap one of the fingers. Then he let Ranu continue with the other nine. Ranu wrapped each toe as well.

Meanwhile, the helpers were carefully wrapping the arms, legs, and body.

Ranu thought they were finished. But then the older helpers placed a *shroud,* like a narrow sheet, over the body. It covered the body from head to toe.

Then the helpers began the wrapping again. They wound the strips of cloth round and round.

When they had wrapped everything for a second time, two men came forward. They had a jar of heated *resin.* With this, they glued the bindings together securely.

"Will the body be wrapped again?" Ranu asked.

"Oh, yes, my boy," said his father's assistant. "There will be 20 layers of shrouds and bindings. When that is done, you will see that this great man's body no longer looks shrunken. He will be about the size he was in life. Or even a little larger."

Ranu's father brought a wooden tray covered with good-luck charms. These were called *shabtis.* They were shaped like small mummies.

Each one held a farm tool. The mummy would need them to work

in the fields of the other world. The assistants began to tuck these shabtis between the layers of wrapping.

"Father," said Ranu. "You said the ba and ka would be able to recognize the body. And they could return to it. I don't see how they can do that. These mummies must look just alike in their wrappings."

"Ah, my son," his father replied. "Later you will understand. Now we will go home. These fine workers will finish their 20 layers of wrapping."

Two days later, Ranu and his father returned to the workshop. The wrappings were finished. The final resin layer had dried.

Ranu walked toward the mummy slowly. He was surprised by what he saw.

The bound head and shoulders were covered by a mask of linen and plaster. The face had been painted in bright colors. Jewels sparkled from the collar at the neck.

"See how much the mask looks like the man who died?" asked Ranu's father. "It is called a portrait mask. Because it is like a picture of the corpse. Now do you see how the ba and the ka could still recognize this body?"

Ranu watched. The body and mask were wrapped one more time. Then his father's helpers painted a last coat of resin over everything.

The carpenters had built a coffin for the mummy. They were decorating it inside and out. They included pictures of gods, goddesses, and magic symbols.

"This fine coffin will protect the mummy," Ranu's father said. "This man was very rich. So he will have a nest of three coffins that fit inside each other. Then the whole thing will go into a stone box. That is called a *sarcophagus.* I don't often embalm anyone this rich. Some men can only afford one coffin."

Not far from the workshop, other men were preparing the rich man's tomb. It had been hollowed out of a cliff. This important man had ordered his tomb built during his lifetime. It was very strong.

Inside were many storage chambers. They were all beautifully carved and decorated. Years before, the walls had been painted with designs.

The paintings showed scenes of what the mummy's life would be like in the new world. For example, servants worked in his fields. Other servants brought him fine foods. And dancers entertained him.

When the tomb was ready, four men carried in a table and chair. Plates, bowls, and musical instruments were added.

A statue of the rich man was in the tomb. If anything happened to the mummy, the ba and ka could come back to rest in the statue.

The mummy was carried into the tomb. Many villagers watched. The women howled and threw dust over their heads. Men sat quietly.

As the procession entered the tomb, Ranu watched a ritual he had sometimes heard about.

It was called the "opening of the mouth." The priests poked at the mouth of the mummy. And they spoke secret words.

They couldn't really open the mouth through 20 layers of wrapping. But the people believed the mummy had magically been given the ability to speak and eat again.

The body was put into the sarcophagus. It was covered with the heavy lid. The jars with the man's organs were arranged nearby.

The body was in place. And family and friends went home. The entrance to the tomb was covered with a wall of huge stone blocks. Everyone hoped the tomb would never be broken into.

The outside of the tomb had a false door. It could not be opened. This was the Egyptian custom. The door was where the ka went in and came out. And the ka was not to be forgotten now. Family members would continue to bring food offerings to the ka. They would leave them just outside the tomb.

Ranu was amazed at all he'd seen. How much he had learned! He could hardly wait to work with his father again. He was proud of his future. His would be important work.

THE GOD ANUBIS

The god Anubis saw to the preparation of bodies. The Egyptians believed that he watched over the embalmers.

Anubis judged the heart of every man who died. He weighed the good deeds against the bad.

The dog, or jackal, was the sacred animal of Anubis. In paintings, he was often shown as a crouching dog. Sometimes the priest at a burial wore a jackal mask to honor Anubis.

The duties of Anubis were much like those of Osiris. Other times he was compared to Thoth.

47

Two Famous Queens

𝓕ew women became queen of ancient Egypt. Hatshepsut and Cleopatra did, however. They lived at very different times. Both were important leaders.

HATSHEPSUT

Around 1495 B.C., King Thutmose I died. He left two children. One was his daughter, Hatshepsut. The other was a son, Thutmose II. To make the family's rule stronger, the sister and brother married each other.

Thutmose II was weak. Hatshepsut was strong-willed and ambitious. More and more, she became the one who made decisions.

After a few years, Thutmose II died. He left a young son who was the child of a harem girl. This boy had the name Thutmose III. But he had no real power. His aunt, Hatshepsut, continued to rule Egypt.

The queen was hard to get along with. She was fierce and warlike. Scribes wrote that she was "a raging crocodile."

But Hatshepsut did good things for Egypt. She sent people on trading trips all along the coast of Africa. Now Egypt had whole new civilizations to trade with.

She built a huge temple at Thebes. And she built other fine buildings as well. Egypt became richer.

When Thutmose III was about 30, Hatshepsut mysteriously disappeared from history. No one knows how she died.

Thutmose III replaced her on the throne. He had her name chiseled off all the buildings. Her statues were smashed. Thutmose III was known as the "Warrior King." He was firmly in charge.

CLEOPATRA

Cleopatra ruled Egypt more than 1,000 years after Hatshepsut.

In those days, many nations had fought wars with the Egyptians. Alexander the Great had swept through Europe. Africa too. Egypt was no longer free.

Cleopatra was of the Ptolemy family. Like Alexander, the Ptolemy family was from Macedon. This was an area north of Greece. When the Ptolemies took over Egypt, they tried to "become" Egyptian.

They wore Egyptian clothes. They worshiped Egyptian gods. And they demanded to be honored the way the other pharaohs had been.

Egypt became rich—but not powerful. Under the Ptolemies, it had no army or navy.

This was not a good time for a nation to be weak. The Roman Empire was expanding. Egypt might be invaded anytime.

Cleopatra knew she must make friends with the Romans. Otherwise, they would overrun Egypt. She got the Roman emperor Julius Caesar to fall in love with her. She even had a son with him.

Caesar was killed in a Roman civil struggle. And Cleopatra turned her attention to Caesar's friend, Mark Antony. They developed a deep love for each other. They had several children.

Finally, Cleopatra could hold off the Romans no longer. Their huge armies were at the very borders of Egypt. Cleopatra made a decision.

It was the custom for defeated rulers to commit suicide. So that is what she would do. According to legend, Cleopatra allowed herself to be bitten by a poisonous snake, a symbol of Egypt.

In 30 B.C., Egypt became a province of the Roman Empire. A 3,000-year-old civilization had ended.

How We've Learned About the Ancient Egyptians

*I*t has been thousands of years since the ancient Egyptians lived. Yet we know much about them. One reason is the very dry climate in which they lived.

Furniture, drawings, and written materials have been preserved under the dry sand of the Nile desert. Paintings on the walls of tombs and pyramids portrayed scenes of everyday life.

The belief in life after death also contributed to what we now know. This belief caused people to fill burial chambers with things they thought they might need in the new life. So tables, chairs, statues, tools, and weapons were preserved.

Many of the things buried were later stolen. But some remained until modern times. From them, historians learned much about Egyptian life.

In recent centuries, two outstanding discoveries have unlocked many secrets of ancient Egypt. They are the Rosetta Stone and the tomb of the young king Tutankhamen.

THE ROSETTA STONE

In 1799, Napoleon was the French emperor. He had been sending his invading armies into Europe and northern Africa. While his armies were marching through Egypt, a French officer discovered something. It was half-buried in the sand near the Nile's delta. And it was at a place called Rosetta.

The amazing discovery turned out to be a large black stone. It was made of *basalt,* a volcanic rock. It was 3' 9" high, 2' 4½" across, and 11" thick.

Part of the top and a section of the right side were missing. The French officer—an engineer—was more interested in the writings he saw on the surface.

Crowded onto every inch of the Rosetta Stone were dozens of tiny letters and pictures. They had been scratched onto the surface.

The writings appeared to have been written three times. The top section was in hieroglyphics. Below that was a section of the same size. It was written in Demotic script. That was a more modern language of Egypt. The bottom third of the stone was written in Greek.

The Rosetta Stone was taken back to France. Scholars were amazed and excited by the discovery. One of them could not rest until he had solved the puzzle of how to read the hieroglyphics. His name was Jean-Francois Champollion.

Ever since his youth, Champollion had been interested in languages. He studied hard in school. He wanted to know all he could about reading and writing all over the world.

His professors had told him about hieroglyphics. They'd said that Egyptian language had been lost in history. That no living person could read it.

Jean-Francois had studied Greek. He'd also studied Coptic, written in the Demotic script. So he was able to read two sections of the Rosetta Stone. That helped a great deal. If he could just figure out the third part of the stone. He'd be the only man in the world to read hieroglyphics!

He knew it would not be easy. The hieroglyphic script has about 750 signs. Most of them are pictures of people, animals, or plants. Some are like little drawings. Some are pictures of what they stand for. Others represent sounds or groups of letters.

Champollion studied the Greek words on the stone first. Then he matched the same words in Demotic.

Sure enough, the message on the stone was repeated three times. Once in each language. He and other experts decided the stone had been written about 196 B.C.

For years, Champollion worked on the messages on the stone. He worked back and forth between Greek and the hieroglyphics.

Finally, he was able to match three letters. He now knew the hieroglyphic symbols for the letters *p*, *l*, and *o*.

On he pushed with his studies. At last, he was able to translate *one word* of the hieroglyphic script. It had taken him 14 years to reach this point.

Once the code was broken, his work went faster. By 1822, Champollion had finished his work. The text on the stone had helped him figure out the hieroglyphic language. Proudly, he published a pamphlet about his discoveries.

Thanks to the Rosetta Stone and Jean-Francois Champollion, scholars could now read ancient Egyptian literature.

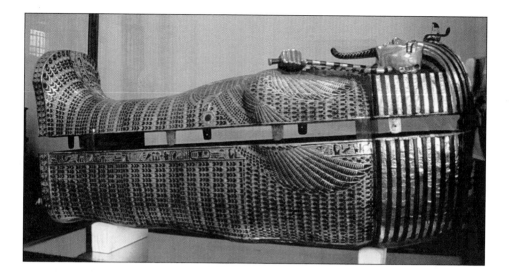

THE TOMB OF TUTANKHAMEN

In 1917, Howard Carter began searching the ruins of the great Valley of the Kings. He was an Egyptologist from England. The valley, near Thebes, had been the site of many large temples and burial vaults.

Carter knew that these burial sites had been robbed over the centuries. He knew, however, that no tomb had ever been found for a young king named Tutankhamen.

For almost six years, Carter and his helpers dug in the sands. They dug through piles of rubble from other tombs and from landslides. The young king's tomb was nowhere to be found.

Carter was ready to give up. His friend, Lord Carnarvon, was paying for the search. He was losing hope too. Finally, Carter asked Carnarvon for just a little more time.

In November 1922, one of Carter's workers found a rock step. It was under piles of rubble. A stairway seemed to lead downward. At the bottom was a sealed entrance.

An excited Carter waited for Carnarvon to arrive in Egypt. Together they would open the tomb.

The two men forced open the doorway. They found an **antechamber** crowded with treasures. There were thrones, stools, chests, and carved boxes heaped to the ceiling.

Statues and chariots crowded the space. The men saw vases, gold jewelry, sandals, bronze trumpets, and ostrich-feather fans.

As they stepped into the burial chamber, they could hardly believe their eyes. Crowded around them were four golden shrines.

Inside the innermost shrine was the sandstone sarcophagus of Tutankhamen. Inside, the young king's mummy was enclosed in a series of three coffins. Willow and olive branches, dry and crumbling, were pressed between the coffins.

Perhaps the greatest surprise was the third coffin. It was made of more than a ton of pure gold! Inside was the mummy itself. Tutankhamen's head was covered in a beautiful golden portrait mask.

The body of the young king was in poor condition. But his organs, which were in four containers in the next room, were better preserved.

Here was one of the greatest finds of all for Egyptologists. Quickly the word about "King Tut" and his wonderful tomb spread around the world.

There were more than 2,000 items in the four rooms of the tomb. This was an exciting discovery.

The questions about Tutankhamen continue today. Historians believe he became king at age eight or nine. They think he was on the throne for only about nine years.

In recent years, some have come to believe Tutankhamen was murdered. Probably by a blow to the head.

The more people study the ancient Egyptians, the more they learn. Discoveries are still being made. Who knows what new knowledge next year will hold!

Glossary

antechamber	an outer room
artisan	a craftsman
bow	the front part of a ship
canal	a waterway
chariot	a two-wheeled horse-drawn cart
corpse	a dead body
dike	a bank of earth built to control water
fertile	rich in material to provide plant growth
hieroglyphics	writing that uses pictures and symbols
kiln	an oven
mummification	the process of creating a mummy
nomads	people who move from place to place
peasant	a laborer
pharaoh	an Egyptian king
reap	to cut
sheaf	a quantity of plants tied together
shepherd's crook	a hooked staff or pole used by shepherds to control animals
shrine	a place to honor a religious figure
sickle	an instrument with a curved blade used for cutting
stern	the back part of a ship
supreme	all-powerful
thresher's flail	a hand tool that has a wooden handle with a short stick hanging from it; used to thresh grain

Index

Aha, 9

Akhenaten, 6

Alexander the Great, 6, 49

ankh, 13

Antony, Mark, 49

Aten, 6

beeswax, 44

Caesar, Julius, 49

Champollion,
Jean-Francois, 52

Cheops, 5, 34, 39

Cleopatra, 6, 48, 49

coffin, 46, 54

craftsmen, 14, 16–18, 35

crops
barley, 19, 21, 25, 31
flax, 19, 22, 31
wheat, 19, 21

cubit, 38

delta, 9, 51

divorce, 26

Djoser, 4, 34

dynasty, 6, 11, 33, 34, 36

Egyptologist, 15, 34, 53, 54

embalmers, 40–47

Eye of Horus, 13, 44

flood, 7–8, 19, 25, 31, 33,
35, 36, 37

gods and goddesses
Amon, 19
Amon-Re, 19
Anubis, 13, 47
Duamutef, 42
Hapy, 42
Hathor, 26
Horus, 13

Imhotep, 34, 36

Imsety, 41

Isis, 12–13

Mut, 19

Osiris, 12–13, 47

Qebhsenuef, 42

Re, 12, 13, 19, 39

Set, 13

Thoth, 16, 47

Great Pyramid, 5, 34–35, 38

Hatshepsut, 5, 48–49

henna, 24

hieroglyphics, 4, 9,
51–52, 55

Hyksos, 5

jewelry, 17, 18, 24, 28,
29, 53

Khephren, 34, 39

Khufu, 34

kingdom, 4–6, 8–9, 10,
14, 20, 38

linen, 22, 24, 28, 42, 44, 45

mask, 17, 41, 42, 45, 47, 54

mastaba, 33

mathematics, 16, 35, 37–38

Mediterranean Sea, 9, 32

Menes, 4, 8–9, 10

Menkaura, 34, 39

mummy, 17, 34, 40–47, 54

Narmer, 9

natron, 41–43

necropolis, 40, 41

Nile River, 4, 7–9, 16, 17,
19, 20, 22, 25, 26, 27,
30–32, 33, 36, 50, 51

ochre, 24

papyrus, 15

priest, 14, 15, 18–19, 41, 47

Ptolemy, 6, 49

Ramses II, 6

Red Sea, 6, 16

resin, 44, 45

Roman Empire, 6, 49

Rosetta Stone, 51–52

sarcophagus, 46, 47, 54

scribe, 9, 14–16, 48

servant, 10, 21, 23, 24, 26,
27, 28, 29, 33, 46

shabtis, 44

shaduf, 26

shrine, 18, 54, 55

shroud, 44

slave, 20, 27

sledge, 35

Snofru, 34

sphinx, 39

Step Pyramid, 4, 34, 36

steward, 21

tax, 15, 19, 31

temple, 13, 18–19, 21, 39,
48, 53

Thutmose I, 5, 48

Thutmose II, 5, 48

Thutmose III, 6, 48

tomb, 16, 19, 26, 32, 33–35,
38, 39, 40, 41, 42, 46, 47,
50, 51, 53–54

Tutankhamen, 6, 51, 53–54